THE POWER OF BRAINSTORMING

The key to generating powerful and original solutions

Written by Nicolas Zinque

Translated by Rebecca Neal

Coaching 50MINUTES.com

INNOVATING AS A TEAM

- **Issue:** how can I set up productive brainstorming sessions in order to arrive at concrete and original decisions?
- **Uses:** innovating as part of a group and finding creative solutions to the company's problems or to its development requirements.
- **Professional context:** all types of groupwork.
- **FAQs:**
  - Can I organise a brainstorming session without a group leader?
  - Can I participate in a brainstorming session if I am the group leader?
  - What is the ideal length of a brainstorming meeting?
  - What is the ideal number of participants?
  - Can I do a brainstorming session remotely?
  - What should I do if nobody is contributing to the discussion?
  - Is it possible to overcome personal conflicts with brainstorming?
  - Is brainstorming suitable for all situations?
  - Is it better to reflect alone or as part of a team?

Since competition and rivalry in a professional setting are tough and merciless, you must always be able to adapt to the demands of your clients. Furthermore, it is necessary – vital, even – for companies to innovate. These transformations can take place through internal reorganisation, the creation of new products, investing in a new niche, etc.

Before committing to one of these changes, it is important to set aside some time for reflection in order to define your objectives and give yourself the means of finding creative and innovative solutions. And what could be better than getting employees to participate in this research? Indeed, teamwork is a strength as well as a necessity: a company cannot rely on the creativity of a single person if it wants to make progress. But how can you best use the creative resources of your team and achieve concrete and innovative advances?

Many people resort to brainstorming: it is a method that everyone knows, or at least thinks they know! It is often seen as an 'ideas fair', during which participants have a lot of fun. However, when it comes to drawing conclusions, the group is often helpless when they have to sort through all the ideas that have been generated. Hours go by, and no concrete decisions are taken! Disillusionment and demotivation set in, as the participants feel as though they have done all that thinking for nothing. You may well have already been in this tricky situation.

However, the method has proven its worth. If mastered, it allows you to tap into the creativity of a whole group and becomes a powerful tool for your company. Despite its image as a relaxed meeting, this method actually requires a great deal of care in its planning and management. Paradoxically, you will motivate your team the most and lead them in the right direction by establishing a precise framework.

> "Brainstorming is identified as a time of greater freedom, whereas the rest of the time our day-to-day work is split

between following guidelines and executing our plans. It is also the time that allows us to align various participants' thoughts so that everyone can make the overall strategy of the company into their own strategy" (Pascal, head of an IT maintenance team for a mutual insurance company).

ORGANISED BRAINSTORMING: THE BASICS

Since it was first used in the 1940s, brainstorming has produced conclusive results. Its creator Alex Osborn (1888-1966), the director of a large American advertising agency, developed the method of the meeting. In doing so, he was trying to respond to the demands of his clients who were looking for creative ideas for their advertising campaigns. Since then the method has evolved and, in proof of its effectiveness, been adopted by a great number of companies.

Brainstorming is based on two premises:

- Each person is gifted with a certain degree of creativity and can be a source of new ideas.
- We tend to not express these ideas, partly out of social conformism, but also because our rational side often quickly comes out on top. Consequently, we must do everything possible to counter this double influence which deforms our ideas.

Logically, brainstorming is also based on a double movement. First of all, 'pure' ideas are gathered, which calls on our creativity, then these ideas are processed rationally, which is based on analysis. This is the foundation of brainstorming, and you should always keep it in mind.

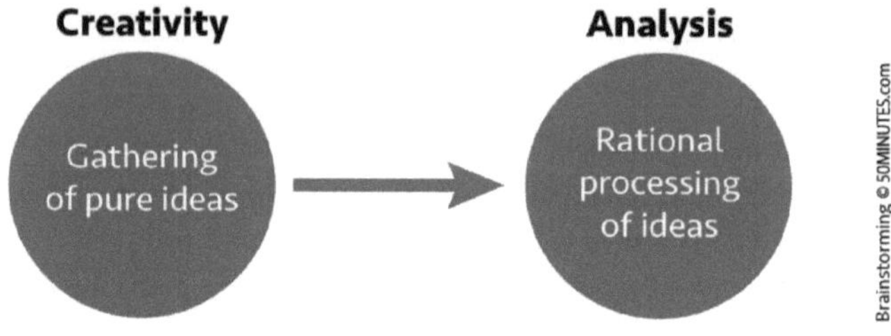

THE GROUP LEADER: THE ARCHITECT OF SUCCESS

The role of the group leader is essential, but often neglected. They are in charge of preparing the brainstorming session, ensuring that it runs smoothly and obtaining the final result. They do not manage the content, but the form: they are therefore not strictly speaking a participant, as they do not put forward ideas. This neutrality is recommended: if you want to occupy this role, this entails withdrawing from the discussion.

During the meeting, the group leader's main tasks are to:

- ensure that the participants fully understand the aim and the issues of the brainstorming session;
- stimulate creativity with the help of different techniques and see that everyone can express themselves;
- get the group back on track if they lose sight of the aim and manage possible conflicts;
- supervise the analysis phase and see that the group se-

lects the most suitable solutions to achieve the aim set;
* see that the time set aside for the meeting is kept to.

The most important qualities of the group leader are observation and listening skills. They must be able to make the group feel comfortable, while at the same time commanding respect. This role may seem difficult at first, but it can be learnt.

PREPARING FOR THE MEETING

Establishing its objective

Behind a brainstorming session, there is an objective to achieve: this can be an idea for a new product, the creation of a new graphic chart which illustrates the company's values, the optimisation of production, etc. If you are working for a client, they generally set the objective themselves. Your mission is then to suggest suitable solutions to them. You should plan the meeting and determine the working methods to be used based on the goal to be reached.

Paradoxically, the more specific you are in your mission statement, the more you will force your team to be creative to overcome the constraints. For example, how can you persuade 20-25 year olds to buy a range of products? How can you establish a particular product in the South?

Putting together the group

The other cornerstone of brainstorming is the group itself. A common error is to call on staff from a single department of the company. Conversely, you should look for participants with varied profiles. For technical innovation, you could bring together designers, engineers, sales representatives, accountants, etc. To return to the example of selling a product to 20-25 year olds, you should include people from this age range in your group. In some circumstances, you will have no choice: the group will be dictated by the clients or by the context of the company (for example, an SME with few employees).

TIPS

- If the object of your brainstorming concerns a client company, invite a representative from this company: in this way, you will improve relations with them and avoid wasting time on off-topic lines of approach.
- Vary the makeup of groups to broaden the reflections, even if working with people who know each other makes interactions easier and lowers inhibitions.
- Avoid inviting a boss, whether or not they are close in the hierarchy, because this can be an impedi-

ment to spontaneity.

Inviting the group

It is now time to invite the group to attend. The participants need to receive practical information and, above all, know the subject of the meeting. If possible, meet them individually to forge an initial connection; if not, invite them by email or phone. In all cases, send a recap email and a reminder the day before. This first approach is an opportunity to invite your group to begin reflecting ahead of time and to gather information. However, do not demand too much preparation or you may impair the spontaneous generation of ideas.

EMAIL INVITATIONS

Use a welcoming tone in your email and slip in a touch of creativity. A simple phrase can be enough to motivate and attune your group.

"I made a habit of starting and ending my invitation with a humorous phrase, often involving wordplay concerning the object of the meeting. Alongside this, the day before a big meeting, I gave my team free time for the last half an hour of the day, on the condition that they used it to think. The next day, I would surprise the group by asking them to present their ideas in an original form" (Thibaut, manager at a telecommunications company)

A suitable location

Just as a caterpillar cannot become a butterfly if it is not surrounded by a protective cocoon, a good group dynamic cannot be achieved unless all the conditions are in place.

Brainstorming will be more productive in a quiet room that is an appropriate size for the group: big enough for everyone to settle themselves comfortably, but not too big, to avoid giving the impression of emptiness. Comfort should be optimum: radiator in winter, air conditioning in summer, toilets close by if possible. Don't forget the most important thing: coffee and other refreshments! On this point, it would seem that water hydrates the brain and stimulates the mind.

Once the location has been chosen, think about arranging the chairs and tables correctly. This is not just a matter of appearances: some layouts encourage participation, whereas others are conducive to a passive information session. To foster dialogue, there are two preferred options:

U-shaped layout	Circular layout
The tables are arranged in a U shape, with the group leader in the centre.	The group leader can be part of the circle, or remain outside it.
Advantage: the visual support used (projector or whiteboard) can be seen by everyone, which makes the transfer of ideas easier.	**Advantage :** there are no blind spots so all the participants can see each other, making this an ideal solution for fostering a group dynamic.
Disadvantage: this layout encourages participants to talk to the group leader rather than to other members of the group.	**Disadvantage:** one of the participants will necessarily have their back to the visual support, which is uncomfortable. Nonetheless, the group leader and their assistant can take this position.

TIP

In an unfamiliar situation, our first reflex is generally to stay with people we know. Feel free to break up pairs of friends and mix people with different profiles. From a creative point of view, by doing this you will bring them into contact with other ways of thinking and other knowledge and skills, and encourage the development of new ideas. From an interpersonal point of view, you will make it easier for employees to meet one another. To do this, assign places in advance by labelling chairs with participants' names.

Working material

During the meeting, all the ideas put forward should be noted down. In order for people to build on other people's suggestions, it is important for them to be permanently visible through some medium. This medium can be electronic, for example a projector linked to a computer, or physical, like a whiteboard or a plain wall, if you are using Post-its.

LEADING A BRAINSTORMING SESSION: GATHERING IDEAS

This is the part where participants have fun – sometimes, too much fun! Their energy must therefore be channelled to lead them in the right direction. If you are well-prepared, this step mainly involves managing the group. From a practical point of view, bringing up and gathering ideas should not take up more than half the meeting, so as to leave time for analysis and decision-making.

The rules of brainstorming

Brainstorming is governed by four principles:

- Suspending all value judgements towards oneself and others. All ideas, including the wildest ones, should be put forward without fear. Spontaneity is the keyword, and this can only reveal itself if each participant feels that they can speak freely.

- Leaving free reign to the imagination, without imposing any constraints.
- Putting forward as many ideas as possible. Their form or content is not that important. The emphasis is on quantity, not necessarily on originality.
- Building on the suggestions of others to combine and improve them.

Memorise these rules, which are the very essence of brainstorming, and teach them to the participants. To achieve this, do not hesitate to stick them up on the walls of the meeting room, summarising them like in the diagram below.

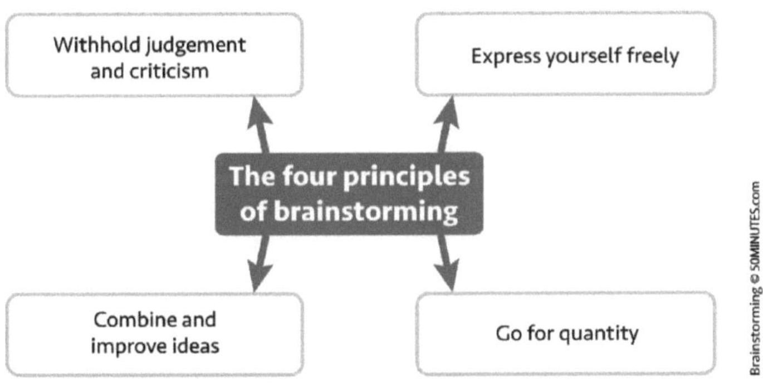

Introduction – get off to a good start

You have warmly welcomed the participants and sat them down in the room. Now, it is time to present the rules of the game to them and get them on board with them. The participants trust the group leader with the choice of creative methods, but the leader must make sure that the way the meeting will run works for everybody. To have a good basis from which to work and/or to avoid any misunderstandings, it is better to spend a few minutes going back over the plan than to be cut off once things are in full swing. The group leader must also confirm the internal rules of the group (breaktime, the possibility of getting up during the meeting to get coffee, etc.).

In your introduction, you must set out:

- **The objective to be reached.** It is not enough to state it: you must also ensure that the group has understood it and that everyone is on the same page, meaning that everyone defines the problem in the same way. To do this, they adopt a common vocabulary. For example, if you want to find solutions directed at 20-25 year olds who smoke 'a lot', first of all you must define precisely what 'a lot' means for the group. Indeed, going around the table will show that this concept is interpreted in a number of different ways: for some people, it means smoking three or four cigarettes per day; for others, it means a packet. If you do not agree on a common threshold together, your brainstorming session is doomed to failure.
- **How the meeting will run,** in other words the amount of time allocated for each stage, the number, duration and time of breaks, etc.
- **The methods to be used.**

Icebreakers

After the introduction, sometimes an icebreaker is needed if the members of the group do not know each other. The aim is to make the participants feel comfortable so that they can express themselves easily. In a way, this is a warm-up.

A FEW EXERCISES

- For the group to get to know each other: in pairs, the participants introduce themselves to their partner, then each person introduces their partner to the group.
- To build team spirit: small physical challenges work very well. In a circle, the participants must pass each other a ball and go around the group as quickly as possible before coming back to their place. Repeat several times to improve performance and develop cohesion.
- To introduce reflection: organise the participants into subgroups of three people and ask them to find a little scenario to resolve a problem (linked to the meeting). Each group then presents their work. Allow around ten minutes for this exercise.

The working method

Before properly beginning the session, leave some time for individual reflection so that each person can immerse themselves in the subject and prepare their initial comments. The method used during the meeting is specified by the group leader while preparing for the brainstorming session, because this takes into account how you are going to bring out the ideas. As each situation has its own specific features, it is important to establish a dialogue with the client or the person who requested the meeting, in order to adapt the method used to the makeup of the group and the company culture.

The most obvious technique is to let the members of the group express themselves when they want to. This method is known as 'spontaneous expression'. As its name suggests, it offers the advantage of encouraging spontaneity and the free flow of speech. However, this process is not well suited to participants who are naturally reserved.

Another very widely used approach is that of going around the table. The group leader gets each participant to speak in turn. Their contribution can include one or more ideas. This method stops a leader from emerging and encourages listening to everybody. The other side of the coin is that it hinders the spontaneity and building on the ideas of other people that are essential to brainstorming. To reduce this problem, you can go around the table and follow this with the spontaneous expression method.

There are other more complex and/or original techniques. You will learn about some of them in the 'Over to you' section.

TIP

In a meeting that is over two hours long, change the method halfway through. In this way, you will stop the group from falling into a creative rut. You can also alternate between spoken and written methods in order to obtain varied ideas and give everyone the opportunity to express themselves.

<u>SOMETHING TO AVOID</u>

Do not spend longer than the allocated time gathering ideas, even if the group is still going. Announce the end of this phase five minutes before and end the session by going around the table and letting everyone express themselves one last time.

Encouraging all members of the group to participate

The major danger of brainstorming is the emergence of leaders who bulldoze the less expressive participants. You must therefore remain attentive to the group dynamic and move towards individuals. Some working methods, such as spontaneous expression, require more frequent intervention on the part of each participant, whereas methods like going around the table naturally distribute speaking time. The Post-its method makes oral expression easier. The trickiest part of winning the trust of participants is encouraging them without pressuring or antagonising them.

> "Some people don't feel as though they have the right to speak, or they think that they have nothing to say. This is of course a mistake, so you have to think about how to appeal to them effectively. Personally, I play on their recognised skills to steer them into commenting on a point that they

initially felt less comfortable with." (Pascal)

If you are afraid of participating in a brainstorming session, know that:

- The fear of being judged is without doubt the main cause of your inhibition. And yet, you need to remember that Alex Osborn created brainstorming precisely to prevent any judgement. Make yourself see the meeting as a safe haven in which you have nothing to lose.
- Expressing your ideas is the best way of showing yourself in a new light and discovering affinities with other colleagues. The more you share, the more you will enjoy the meeting.
- Do not see brainstorming as a competition, but as the carrying out of a collective task. The aim is not to choose somebody's idea, but to build the best project possible thanks to collective creativity. To do this, you need to be attentive to the other participants.

TAKING NOTES

During the meeting, all the suggestions should be recorded and be permanently visible to encourage people to build on others' ideas. Watch out: the assistant who is taking notes must write them down as they are put forward, refraining from any judgement. Sometimes a single word is enough to change the meaning of an idea!

This intense session of creativity must then give way to rationality. Although the analysis phase allows you to determine the success of your gathering of ideas, it is nonetheless often neglected. There is no point having hundreds of ideas if none of them become reality. Dedicate at least half the meeting, and no less, to this!

From criticism (understood here in a positive and constructive sense) of the ideas put forward during the meeting, there emerges a series of selection criteria to develop a validation method. Like in your general introduction, set out your working methods and have the group agree on them. This phase risks provoking discussions and, sometimes, tensions. This is another aspect of group management that the group leader must be able to deal with.

Criteria for the validation of ideas

Determining selection criteria allows you to justify the idea you end up choosing. Once again, everybody needs to be on the same page so that ideas can be compared fairly. In practice, the criteria are not necessarily defined by the team, because the client often fixes their own demands.

To establish these criteria, you must return to the initial question. The first stage involves withdrawing suggestions that are clearly off-topic with regard to this question.

In a second phase, you must define criteria that are specific to your subject, in order to differentiate between the suggestions. You must also determine which criteria carry the most weight.

In our example 'how can we convince 20-25 year olds to buy a range of products?', the effectiveness of the solution depends on criteria such as originality (has this solution already been implemented by a competitor?), the life cycle of this audience (they are often students, whose years are marked by exams in December-January, May-June and August, summer jobs, etc.) and the places they visit (student clubs, websites and forums for young people, etc.), the ability to act over the long term or, conversely, to generate buzz by riding the wave of current events, etc.

Finally, we must add feasibility criteria to this: ask the different professions to eliminate the solutions that they believe are impossible to carry out in their area of expertise. For example, some suggestions may be unrealistic from the point of view of physics, IT, etc. It goes without saying that, if the quality is the same, the solutions that are the least onerous and the easiest to implement will win out. This is known as profitability criteria.

The selection method

Once the selection criteria have been identified, all that remains it to apply them to the suggestions put forward. But how should you go about this? There are two methods worth considering:

- **Voting:** each idea is voted on, in accordance with the

established criteria. Counting up the points produces a hierarchy of solutions.

- **Consensus:** the participants discuss and agree on the chosen solutions. This method takes more time, but has the advantage of being less mechanical than voting. Furthermore, it encourages the group to agree with the result.

Applying the chosen ideas

The idea which has received the most votes or been chosen by consensus must now be realised. The decision is therefore not an endpoint, but another starting point: the starting point for the application of the solution. You must now determine your new goals, list the tasks to be carried out, name the people in charge of it and put together the team, set the schedule and define the budget. In reality, the adventure that began with your brainstorming will only come to a close when the project is being evaluated, in other words after the new guidelines have been integrated.

Once the workshop is finished, do not forget to make someone responsible for following up on the ideas put forward (the project manager, for example). This person should provide all the participants in the meeting with feedback in the following weeks and months. Even if some members of the group are not involved with the later stages, they all deserve to be informed of the success of their project.

The other benefits of brainstorming

As well as encouraging the development of creative tailored solutions, brainstorming has other advantages. It enables:

- the strengthening of interprofessional connections and of cooperation within a group, because all team members feel that they are fully integrated in the undertaking (team-building);
- the stimulation of each employee's reflective and crea-

tive capacities;
- the exchange of knowledge and the sharing of skills;
- professional effectiveness;
- self-assertion within a group.

TOP TIPS

- **Be structured:** create a recap sheet containing every stage of your meeting and the time allocated for each one. All this information will be given at the start of the meeting.
- **Rehearse your introduction at home:** a lack of structure will dent your credibility and send a negative message to the group. Similarly, have a look around the meeting room the day before to make sure that everything is in order.
- **Set an optimistic example to your group:** a brainstorming session is an interpersonal exchange which will work much better if there is a good atmosphere. Sometimes, a few words or a smile are all that is needed to encourage a discussion.
- **Be creative when setting up the brainstorming session:** if you work with the same group several times, vary your methods and materials so as to avoid creative ruts. Do not hesitate to combine several methods during the same meeting.
- **Keep to a strict framework:** in-depth debates should only take place during the analysis phase. Be careful, because the participants will be tempted to discuss the practical aspects of some of the ideas put forward during the gathering phase.
- **Write up minutes and take care to preserve a record of your meetings:** you will use them later on to develop new ideas.
- **Transform the joint session into a team-building**

exercise: brainstorming is a fun time at work. It enables your company's employees to bond with one another. Encourage them to see each other again outside this meeting. Why not organise drinks to celebrate reaching your goal?

- **Make brainstorming part of the company culture:** encourage participants to exchange ideas over coffee, for example. The conditions will not always be optimal, but creativity will always be stimulated.
- **Keep in mind that brainstorming is one of many tools:** by making it part of a structured method, you will make it even more powerful. It is part of what is known today as 'creativity management', which brings together all the tools which encourage creation in a company.

FAQS

CAN I ORGANISE A BRAINSTORMING SESSION WITHOUT A GROUP LEADER?

Unless all the members of the group know each other incredibly well and are very experienced in the subject, then no. The group leader is at the heart of the brainstorming session, like the conductor of an orchestra. They are an indispensable authority figure with regard to the form (and not the content) of the session.

CAN I PARTICIPATE IN A BRAINSTORMING SESSION IF I AM THE GROUP LEADER?

This double role is not recommended, for the simple and good reason that the group leader needs a certain distance. Furthermore, this raises the question of neutrality, particularly in a group that you do not know: your interventions could be seen as promoting your personal ideas.

WHAT IS THE IDEAL LENGTH OF A BRAINSTORMING MEETING?

The length depends on a number of factors, such as the subject to be dealt with, the number of participants, etc. The most important thing is to make sure you divide the phases appropriately: allow between fifteen and thirty minutes for the group to settle in and introduce themselves. After that, the creative phase is always shorter than the processing of ideas. The ideal length of a brainstorming session is between two and three hours. Any shorter and you will be rushing; any longer and the attention of the group will flag. Respect the formula 'introduction time + collection of ideas ≤ analysis time'.

WHAT IS THE IDEAL NUMBER OF PARTICIPANTS?

Between five and eight: below this range the discussion risks lacking depth and breadth; above it the group will become difficult to manage. For between nine and twenty people, organise parallel brainstorming sessions in several groups, and intersperse them with periods of pooling ideas together. For more than twenty participants, use techniques for organising large groups, such as the Phillips 6.6 method (groups of six people discuss an issue for six minutes). In this case too, you can organise parallel brainstorming sessions interspersed with the pooling of ideas.

CAN I DO A BRAINSTORMING SESSION REMOTELY?

Absolutely. The development of communication technologies has encouraged the emergence of remote brainstorming. It puts people who are geographically distant, but working for the same multinational, for example, in contact with one another. Remote brainstorming can take two forms:

- Videoconference brainstorming. The group discusses in

real time via long-distance communication software.
- Brainstorming using a 'wiki' type application. Written exchanges take place on a shared platform. In this case, the collection of ideas and the analysis do not necessarily happen in real time: each person can have a longer time to react.

WHAT SHOULD I DO IF NOBODY IS CONTRIBUTING TO THE DISCUSSION?

At the start of the meeting, it is unlikely that nobody has any ideas; most probably, nobody wants to express them. In the first case, this can be due to embarrassment or awkwardness. To resolve this, try an icebreaker. If, on the contrary, nobody wants to speak, the problem is more serious: is it an interpersonal conflict? A bad atmosphere? You must identify this problem and resolve it immediately.

During the meeting, you could be faced with a lull in the discussion. In this case, the role of the group leader is to elicit more contributions from the group. Here are some solutions:

- return to the initial topic;
- reread the ideas that have already been put forward and possibly ask for clarification on them;
- take external documentation (internet searches, audio-visual documents, clients' opinions, etc.) as your starting point;
- change your method.

IS IT POSSIBLE TO OVERCOME PERSONAL CONFLICTS WITH BRAINSTORMING?

Brainstorming encourages cohesion and can allow people to discover affinities. Nonetheless, it is not strictly speaking a method of conflict resolution. If two people dislike each other, it is better to deal with the issue before the meeting, via mediation.

IS BRAINSTORMING SUITABLE FOR ALL SITUATIONS?

It works in almost all situations, but can prove ineffective in some cases. When individuals are too far away from each other in the hierarchy (in large companies, for example), they may be reluctant to open up completely. Some brainstorming methods are not suitable for all contexts: for example, roleplaying requires the right state of mind. If you do not know the group well, avoid overly original methods to start with.

IS IT BETTER TO REFLECT ALONE OR AS PART OF A TEAM?

Within the framework of group innovation, this is a legitimate question, as different specialists have different takes on the subject. For example, some studies, listed in *Le groupe est-il plus créatif que l'individu isolé ? Le cas du brainstorming : 1953-2003, cinquante ans de recherche* ['Is the group more creative than the isolated individual? The case of brainstorming: fifty years of research 1953-2003'] by

Valentine Galtier and Éva Delacroix, maintain that thinking alone is more effective and leads to a greater number of original solutions. If you are alone you will be less distracted and will not waste time in off-topic discussions. However, others believe that it is precisely the exchange of ideas which gives brainstorming its richness: building on the ideas of other people is one of the four essential rules. Finally, there is nothing stopping you from bringing together the advantages of individual work and teamwork by organising these two phases as part of your meeting!

OVER TO YOU

Every situation has its own method for collecting ideas.

The different brainstorming methods

Method	How it works	Number of participants	Duration
Post-its	The participants write down their ideas on Post-it notes and stick them on a wall. Initially, let them think and organise their papers in the time given. Next, take the time to read all the suggestions put forward, before moving on to spontaneous expression. This method is a lot of fun and is one of the most popular approaches. It allows ideas to be assembled visually by moving the Post-its, and makes sorting easier. To prepare for the analysis phase, ask the participants to organise all the ideas thematically.	3-8 people	20-30 minutes to take notes on Post-its, then 30 minutes of spontaneous expression
Role-playing	There are several variants, but the principle is as follows: the participants take on a role and a way of thinking that is different from their own. For a less advanced approach, you can simply ask the question "What would this company, this figure, this client do in this situation?" You can also simply change an aspect of the person: age, nationality, etc. This method needs a particular state of mind in the group, or it will turn into a joke. Some people do not like this technique as they find it somewhat theatrical.	3-8 people	10 minutes to prepare, then 20-50 minutes to role-play

Method	How it works	Number of participants	Duration
Opposite thinking	The principle is to think back to front by reversing the question. Rather than asking yourself "How can I meet my clients' expectations?", ask yourself "How can I not meet their expectations?" Then all you have to do is reverse these negative ideas to make them positive! Although it may seem absurd at first, this method is very refreshing.	2-8 people	20-30 minutes
6-3-5 brainwriting	This method takes its name from its principles: six people each write three ideas on a blank sheet of paper. After five minutes, the notes are passed on to the next person and the cycle starts again: five minutes to write down three ideas, but this time building on the ideas already written on the sheet. In practice, you can alter the parameters of brainwriting, add participants, increase the thinking time, etc. Although it limits spontaneity somewhat, this method is very effective with a group that struggles to express itself orally.	4-8 people	20-40 minutes
Mind map	The aim is to establish a visual and semantic connection between the problem and the solutions put forward. It is a form of 'creative structuring'. The central issue is placed in the middle of the document. The ideas put forward are added to it and, as the exercise progresses, are arranged into categories. Nowadays, mind mapping is usually carried out with the help of software, some of which is free (MindMap, Xmind, FreeMind, etc.).	3-8 people	30-50 minutes

FURTHER READING

BIBLIOGRAPHY

- Bachelet, R. (2012) Animer un brainstorming. *Gestion de projet*. [Online]. [Accessed 8 November 2016]. Available from: <http://gestiondeprojet.pm/animer-un-brainstorming/>
- De Brabandère, L. (2004) *Le management des idées. De la créativité à l'innovation*. Paris: Dunod.
- DeCenzo, D., Gabilliet, P. and Robbins, S. (2008) *Management. L'essentiel des concepts et des pratiques*. Paris: Pearson Education.
- Delacroix, E. and Galiter, V (2005) Le groupe est-il plus créatif que l'individu isolé ? Le cas du brainstorming : 1953-2003, cinquante ans de recherche. *Management & Avenir*. 2(4), pp. 71-86. [Online]. [Accessed 8 November 2016]. Available from: <http://www.cairn.info/revue-management-et-avenir-2005-2-page-71.htm>
- Maccio, C. (1995) *Des réunions plus efficaces*. Lyon: Chroniques sociales.
- McCurdy, R. (2013) *Faire ensemble. Outils participatifs pour le collectif*. Corcelle: Passerelle Éco.
- Osborn, A. (1953) *Applied Imagination: Principles and Procedures of Creative Problem Solving*. New York: Charles Scribner's Sons.
- Sorez, H. (1977), *Pour conduire une réunion*. Paris: Éditions Hatier.

ADDITIONAL SOURCES

- BoostCompanies (No date) *23 creativity killers that will drown any brainstorming session*. [Online]. [Accessed 8 November 2016]. Available from: <https://boostcompanies.com/creativity-killers/>
- Clark, C. (1989) *Brainstorming: How to Create Successful Ideas*. California: Wilshire Book Company.
- Cotton, D. (2016) *The Smart Solution Book: 68 Tools for Brainstorming, Problem-Solving and Decision-Making*. Edinburgh: Pearson Education Limited.
- Curedale, R.A. (2013) *50 Brainstorming Methods: For Team and Individual Ideation*. California: Design Community College Inc.
- Isaksen, S., Dorval, B. and Treffinger, D. (2010) *Creative Approaches to Problem Solving: A Framework for Innovation and Change*. California: SAGE Publications.
- Wilson, C. (2013) *Brainstorming and Beyond: A User-Centered Design Method*. Oxford: Elsevier Inc.